How to Use This PLANNER

There are many aspects to a crafter's process. Organization, planning, and execution all require multiple steps, and it can be difficult to keep track of everything. This planner will help you do just that.

In the first section, you will find pages to log your craft budgets, your current measurements, and all the goals you've completed over time. The next section is a glossary, where you can learn new terms and their helpful abbreviations. The final section is devoted to your projects, giving you space to record everything from the materials you used, your satisfaction with the final result, any changes you made to the pattern, and more.

This planner is meant to work for you, whether you are the most experienced crafter you know, or just starting out with your first project.

Contents

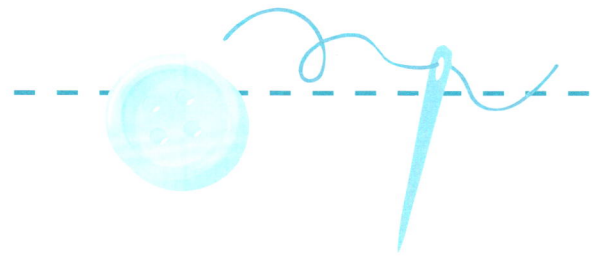

Craft Planner is a new work, first published by
Dover Publications in 2024.

ISBN-13: 978-0-486-85249-2
ISBN-10: 0-486-85249-0

Manufactured in China
85249001   2024
www.doverpublications.com

Goal Tracker

Your goal should be something you aspire to complete related to your crafting. This could be anything from a number of projects you want to complete to a new craft you want to learn. Write this in pencil, as our goals often change as we go.

Date	Goal	Progress
mm/dd/yy	Learn how to chain crochet	Completed

Goal Tracker

Your goal should be something you aspire to complete related to your crafting. This could be anything from a number of projects you want to complete to a new craft you want to learn. Write this in pencil, as our goals often change as we go.

Date	Goal	Progress

Goal Tracker

Your goal should be something you aspire to complete related to your crafting. This could be anything from a number of projects you want to complete to a new craft you want to learn. Write this in pencil, as our goals often change as we go.

Date	Goal	Progress

Goal Tracker

Your goal should be something you aspire to complete related to your crafting. This could be anything from a number of projects you want to complete to a new craft you want to learn. Write this in pencil, as our goals often change as we go.

Date	Goal	Progress

Goal Tracker

Your goal should be something you aspire to complete related to your crafting. This could be anything from a number of projects you want to complete to a new craft you want to learn. Write this in pencil, as our goals often change as we go.

Date	Goal	Progress

Measurements

On this page, you should write your current measurements in pencil. Our bodies change constantly, so every few months, you should check these measurements to make sure they are accurate.

Body Measurement Chart

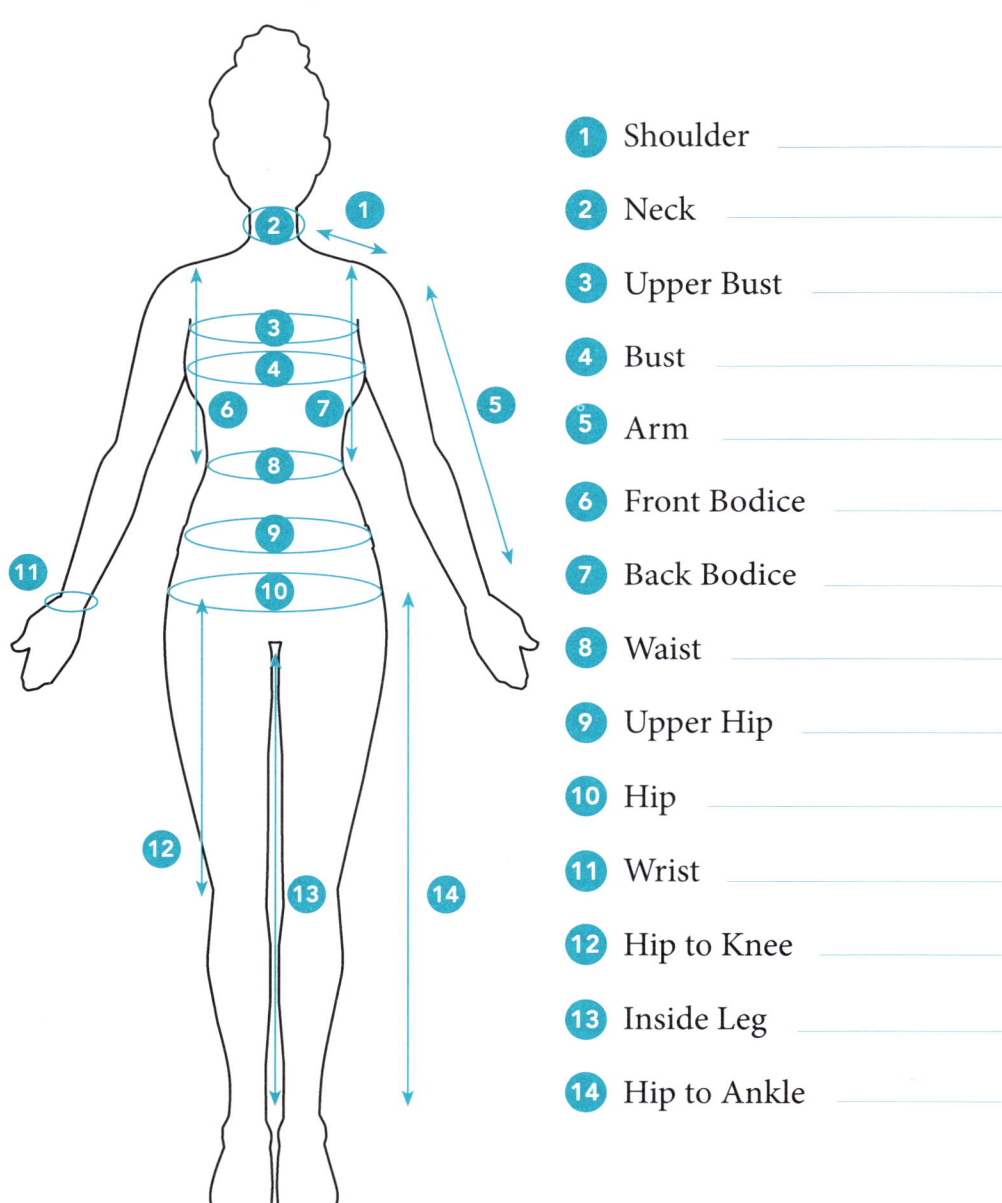

1. Shoulder _____
2. Neck _____
3. Upper Bust _____
4. Bust _____
5. Arm _____
6. Front Bodice _____
7. Back Bodice _____
8. Waist _____
9. Upper Hip _____
10. Hip _____
11. Wrist _____
12. Hip to Knee _____
13. Inside Leg _____
14. Hip to Ankle _____

Measurements

On this page, you should write your current measurements in pencil. Our bodies change constantly, so every few months, you should check these measurements to make sure they are accurate.

Body Measurement Chart

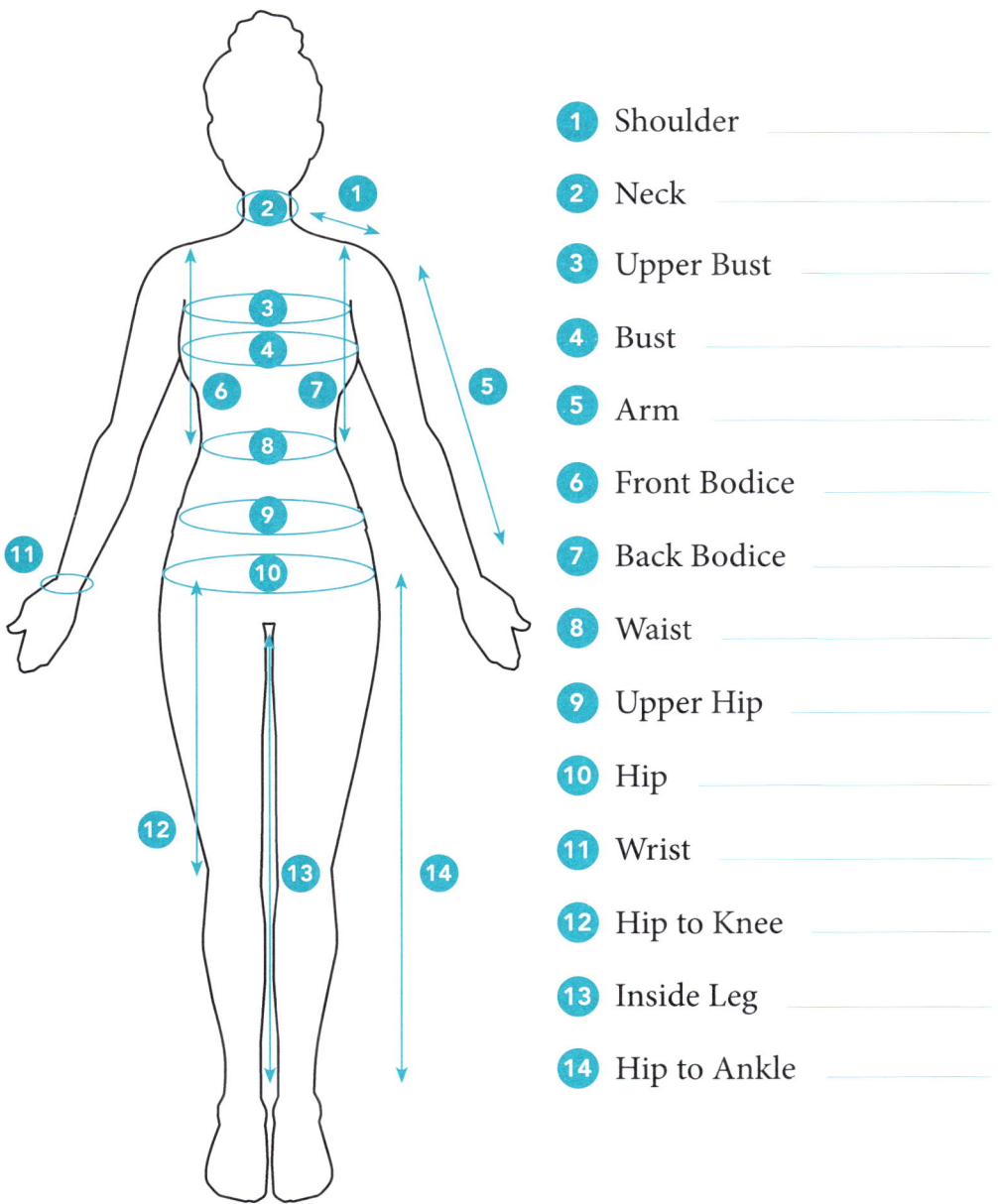

1. Shoulder ⎯⎯⎯⎯⎯⎯
2. Neck ⎯⎯⎯⎯⎯⎯
3. Upper Bust ⎯⎯⎯⎯⎯⎯
4. Bust ⎯⎯⎯⎯⎯⎯
5. Arm ⎯⎯⎯⎯⎯⎯
6. Front Bodice ⎯⎯⎯⎯⎯⎯
7. Back Bodice ⎯⎯⎯⎯⎯⎯
8. Waist ⎯⎯⎯⎯⎯⎯
9. Upper Hip ⎯⎯⎯⎯⎯⎯
10. Hip ⎯⎯⎯⎯⎯⎯
11. Wrist ⎯⎯⎯⎯⎯⎯
12. Hip to Knee ⎯⎯⎯⎯⎯⎯
13. Inside Leg ⎯⎯⎯⎯⎯⎯
14. Hip to Ankle ⎯⎯⎯⎯⎯⎯

Measurements

On this page, you should write your current measurements in pencil. Our bodies change constantly, so every few months, you should check these measurements to make sure they are accurate.

Body Measurement Chart

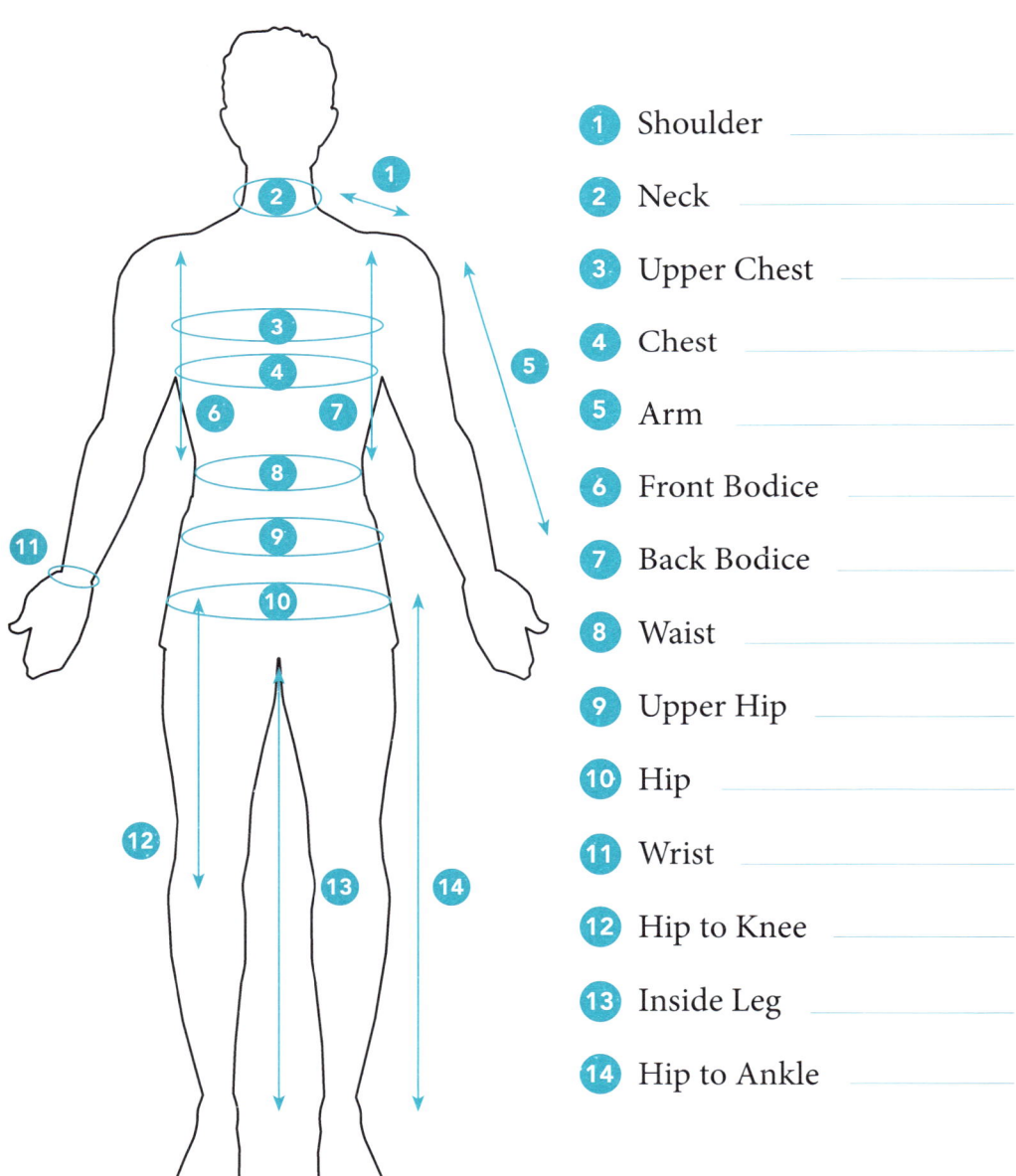

1. Shoulder _____
2. Neck _____
3. Upper Chest _____
4. Chest _____
5. Arm _____
6. Front Bodice _____
7. Back Bodice _____
8. Waist _____
9. Upper Hip _____
10. Hip _____
11. Wrist _____
12. Hip to Knee _____
13. Inside Leg _____
14. Hip to Ankle _____

Measurements

On this page, you should write your current measurements in pencil. Our bodies change constantly, so every few months, you should check these measurements to make sure they are accurate.

Body Measurement Chart

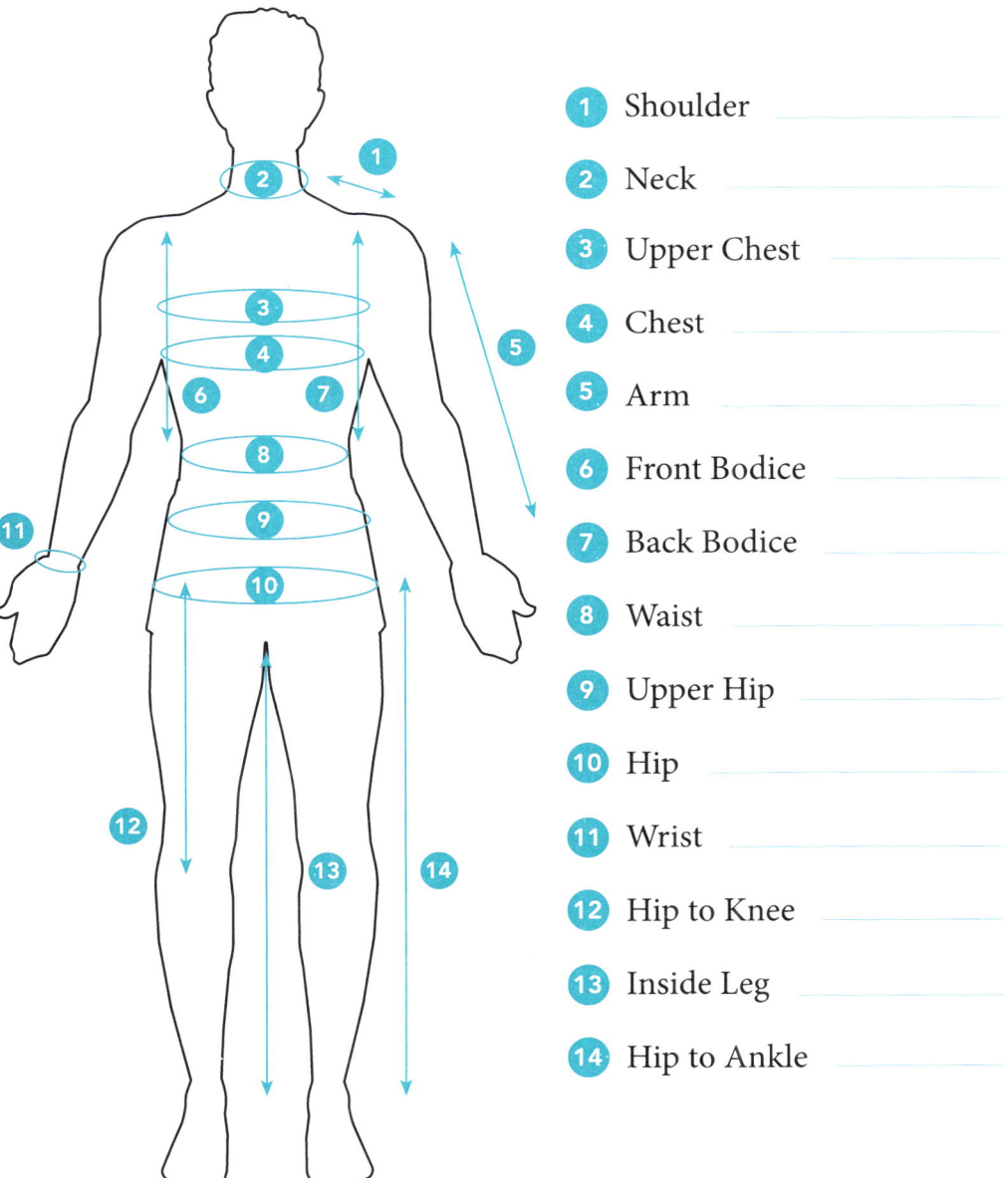

1. Shoulder _____
2. Neck _____
3. Upper Chest _____
4. Chest _____
5. Arm _____
6. Front Bodice _____
7. Back Bodice _____
8. Waist _____
9. Upper Hip _____
10. Hip _____
11. Wrist _____
12. Hip to Knee _____
13. Inside Leg _____
14. Hip to Ankle _____

Budget Tracker

When keeping track of your budget, it is good to remember not only what you bought, but why. If you bought a beautiful fabric but don't have a project in mind, consider acquiring a pattern before buying more material.

Date	Category	Product	Price
mm/dd/yy	Yarn	Organic Cotton Yarn in Blue from X Brand	$5.99

Total Spent: _____

Budget Tracker

When keeping track of your budget, it is good to remember not only what you bought, but why. If you bought a beautiful fabric but don't have a project in mind, consider acquiring a pattern before buying more material.

Date	Category	Product	Price

Total Spent: _____

Budget Tracker

When keeping track of your budget, it is good to remember not only what you bought, but why. If you bought a beautiful fabric but don't have a project in mind, consider acquiring a pattern before buying more material.

Date	Category	Product	Price

Total Spent: _____

Budget Tracker

When keeping track of your budget, it is good to remember not only what you bought, but why. If you bought a beautiful fabric but don't have a project in mind, consider acquiring a pattern before buying more material.

Date	Category	Product	Price

Total Spent: _____

Budget Tracker

When keeping track of your budget, it is good to remember not only what you bought, but why. If you bought a beautiful fabric but don't have a project in mind, consider acquiring a pattern before buying more material.

Date	Category	Product	Price

Total Spent: _____

Budget Tracker

When keeping track of your budget, it is good to remember not only what you bought, but why. If you bought a beautiful fabric but don't have a project in mind, consider acquiring a pattern before buying more material.

Date	Category	Product	Price

Total Spent: _____

Budget Tracker

When keeping track of your budget, it is good to remember not only what you bought, but why. If you bought a beautiful fabric but don't have a project in mind, consider acquiring a pattern before buying more material.

Date	Category	Product	Price

Total Spent: _____

Budget Tracker

When keeping track of your budget, it is good to remember not only what you bought, but why. If you bought a beautiful fabric but don't have a project in mind, consider acquiring a pattern before buying more material.

Date	Category	Product	Price

Total Spent: _____

Budget Tracker

When keeping track of your budget, it is good to remember not only what you bought, but why. If you bought a beautiful fabric but don't have a project in mind, consider acquiring a pattern before buying more material.

Date	Category	Product	Price

Total Spent: _____

Glossary

Crocheting

al	alternate
approx	approximately
beg	begin/beginning
bet	between
bl or blo	back loop or back loop only
bo	bobble
bp	back post
bpdc	back post double crochet
bpdtr	back post double treble crochet
bphdc	back post half double crochet
bpsc	back post single crochet
bpdc	back post double crochet
bptc	back post treble crochet
cc	contrasting color
ch	chain stitch
ch-	refer to chain or space made by chain row
ch-sp	chain space
cl	cluster

cont	continue
dc	double crochet
dc2tog	double crochet two stitches together
dec(s)	decrease(s)
dtr	double treble crochet
edc	extended double crochet
ehdc	extended half double crochet
esc	extended single crochet
etr	extended treble crochet
fl or flo	front loop or front loop only
foll	following
fp	front post
fpdc	front post double crochet
fpdtr	front post double treble crochet
fphdc	front post half double crochet
fpsc	front post single crochet
fptr	front post treble crochet
hdc	half double crochet
hdc2tog	half double crochet two stitches together

Crocheting

inc	increase
lp	loop
m	marker
mc	main color
pat/patt	pattern
pc	popcorn stitch
pm	place marker
prev	previous
ps or puff	puff stitch
re	remaining
rep	repeat
rnd	round
rs	right side
sc	single crochet
sc2tog	single crochet two stitches together
sh	shell
sk	skip
sl st	slip stitch
sm or sl m	slip marker

sp	space
st	stitch
tbl	through back loop
tch	turning chain
tog	together
tr	treble crochet
tr2tog	treble crochet two stitches together
trtr	triple treble crochet
ws	wrong side
yo	yarn over
yoh	yarn over hook
*	repeat instructions following the single asterisk as directed
* *	repeat instructions between asterisks as many times as directed or repeat at specified locations within row, stitch, or pattern
{ }	work instructions within brackets as many times as directed
[ ]	work instructions within brackets as many times as directed
( )	work instructions within parentheses as many times as directed or work a group of stitches all in the same stitch or space

alt	alternate
beg	beginning
block	the process of washing and pulling a piece before pinning it down to dry into a new shape
byo	backward yarn over
cc	contrasting color
cn	cable needle
CO	cast on/cast off
cont	continue
dec(s)	decrease(s)
dpn	double-pointed needles
inc(s)	increase(s)
k	knit
k1b	knit stitch in the row below
kfb	knit into the front and back of a stitch, acts as an increase
ksp	knit a stitch, slip the stitch from right needle to left, pass second stitch on left needle over the first stitch on the needle and off the needle, return stitch to right needle

k2tog	knit two together, one right-leaning decrease
kwise	knitwise
LH	left hand
lp	loop
m	marker
mc	main color
p	purl
pat/patt	pattern
pfb	purl into front and back of a stitch; single purl increase
pm	place markers
p2tog	purl two stitches together; single decrease
prev	previous
psso	pass slipped stitch over
p2sso	pass two slipped stitches over
pwise	purlwise
rem	remaining
rep	repeat
rev st	reverse stockinette
RH	right hand

rnd	round
RS	right side
skp	slip one knitwise, knit one, pass slip stitch over knit stitch; single left-leaning decrease
sk2p	slip one knitwise, knit two together, pass slip stitch over knit two together; double left-leaning decrease
sl	slip
sl1k	slip one knitwise
sl1p	slip one purlwise
sl st	slip stitch
sm	slip marker
ssk	slip two stitches knitwise, knit those two stitches together through the back loops; single left-leaning decrease
ssp	slip two stitches knitwise, return these two stitches to the left needle, purl those two stitches together through the back loops; single left-leaning decrease
sssk	slip three stitches knitwise, knit those three stitches together through the back loops; single left-leaning decrease

sssp	slip three stitches knitwise, return these three stitches to the left needle, purl those three stitches together through the back loops; single left-leaning decrease
s2kp2	slip two stitches as if going to k2tog, knit one, pass two slipped stitches over knit stitch; centered double decrease
sspp2	slip two stitches knitwise, return these stitches to left needle, then slip them as if to p2tog through back loops, purl one, pass two slipped stitches over purl stitch; centered double decrease
st	stitch
st st	stockinette stitch
tbl	through back loop
tfl	through front loop
tog	together
ws	wrong side
w&t	wrap and turn
wyib	with yarn in back
wyif	with yarn in front
yb	yarn back
yfwd or yf	yarn forward
yo	yarn over
yon	yarn over needle
yrn	yarn round needle

Sewing

a/h	armhole
b/l	bustline
b/p	bust point
cb	center back
cbf	center back fold
cbl	cross back line
cf	center front
cff	center front fold
ch	crown height (sleeves)
clr	collar
drs	dress
e/l	elbow line
fcng	facing
gl	grainline
h/l	hipline
jkt	jacket
k/l	knee line
lhsaw	left-hand side as worn
nck	neck

ol	overlock [serge]
rhsaw	right-hand side as worn
rs	right side
rsd	right side down
rst	right sides together
s/b	side back
s/f	side front
sa	seam allowance
shldr or sh	shoulder
sk	skirt
slv	sleeve
ss	side seam
tp	top
tr	trousers
u/l	underarm line
w/band	waistband
wl	waistline
ws	wrong side
wsd	wrong side down
wst	wrong sides together
zz	zigzag stitch

Project Planner

Craft Type: ....

....

Pattern: ....

....

Materials List:

....
....
....
....
....
....

Date Started: ....

Date Ended: ....

Difficulty Level:

Beginner   Advanced

◯   ◯   ◯   ◯   ◯

Picture:

Notes:

....
....
....
....
....
....
....
....
....

Review:

....
....
....
....
....
....

Would Do Again:

Yes ◯   No ◯   Maybe ◯

Progress Tracker:

▶

Project Planner

Craft Type: ....
....

Pattern: ....
....

Materials List:
....
....
....
....
....
....

Notes:
....
....
....
....
....
....
....
....
....
....

Progress Tracker:

Date Started: ....
Date Ended: ....

Difficulty Level:

Beginner   Advanced

○ ○ ○ ○ ○

Picture:

Review:
....
....
....
....
....

Would Do Again:

Yes ○   No ○   Maybe ○

Project Planner

Craft Type: ....

....

Pattern: ....

....

Materials List:

....
....
....
....
....
....
....

Date Started: ....

Date Ended: ....

Difficulty Level:

Beginner   Advanced

◯   ◯   ◯   ◯   ◯

Picture:

Notes:

....
....
....
....
....
....
....
....
....
....
....

Review:

....
....
....
....
....
....

Would Do Again:

Yes ◯   No ◯   Maybe ◯

Progress Tracker:

Project Planner

Craft Type: ....
....

Pattern: ....
....

Date Started: ....

Date Ended: ....

Difficulty Level:

Beginner   Advanced

◯ ◯ ◯ ◯ ◯

Materials List:

....
....
....
....
....
....
....

Picture:

Notes:

....
....
....
....
....
....
....
....
....
....
....

Review:

....
....
....
....
....
....

Would Do Again:

Yes ◯   No ◯   Maybe ◯

Progress Tracker:

▶

Project Planner

Craft Type: ....
....

Pattern: ....
....

Materials List:
....
....
....
....
....
....
....

Date Started: ....

Date Ended: ....

Difficulty Level:

Beginner   Advanced

◯ ◯ ◯ ◯ ◯

Picture:

Notes:
....
....
....
....
....
....
....
....
....
....
....

Review:
....
....
....
....
....
....

Would Do Again:

Yes ◯   No ◯   Maybe ◯

Progress Tracker:

Project Planner

Craft Type: ....

....

Pattern: ....

....

Materials List:

....
....
....
....
....
....

Difficulty Level:

Beginner   Advanced

◯ ◯ ◯ ◯ ◯

Picture:

Notes:

....
....
....
....
....
....
....
....
....
....
....

Review:

....
....
....
....
....

Would Do Again:

Yes ◯   No ◯   Maybe ◯

Progress Tracker:

▶

Project Planner

Craft Type: ....
....

Pattern: ....
....

Materials List:
....
....
....
....
....
....
....

Date Started: ....

Date Ended: ....

Difficulty Level:

Beginner   Advanced

◯ ◯ ◯ ◯ ◯

Picture:

Notes:
....
....
....
....
....
....
....
....
....
....

Review:
....
....
....
....
....
....

Would Do Again:

Yes ◯   No ◯   Maybe ◯

Progress Tracker:

Project Planner

Craft Type: ....

....

Pattern: ....

....

Difficulty Level:

Beginner   Advanced

◯ ◯ ◯ ◯ ◯

Materials List:

....

....

....

....

....

....

....

Picture:

Notes:

....

....

....

....

....

....

....

....

....

....

....

....

Review:

....

....

....

....

....

....

Would Do Again:

Yes ◯   No ◯   Maybe ◯

Progress Tracker:

Project Planner

Craft Type: ....

Pattern: ....

....

Date Started: ....

Date Ended: ....

Difficulty Level:

Beginner   Advanced

◯ ◯ ◯ ◯ ◯

Materials List:

....
....
....
....
....
....
....

Picture:

Notes:

....
....
....
....
....
....
....
....
....
....
....

Review:

....
....
....
....
....

Would Do Again:

Yes ◯   No ◯   Maybe ◯

Progress Tracker:

▶

Project Planner

Craft Type: ....

....

Pattern: ....

....

Date Started: ....

Date Ended: ....

Difficulty Level:

Beginner   Advanced

◯ ◯ ◯ ◯ ◯

Materials List:

....

....

....

....

....

....

Picture:

Notes:

....

....

....

....

....

....

....

....

....

....

Review:

....

....

....

....

....

....

Would Do Again:

Yes ◯   No ◯   Maybe ◯

Progress Tracker:

▶

Project Planner

Craft Type: ....
....

Pattern: ....
....

Difficulty Level:

Beginner   Advanced

◯ ◯ ◯ ◯ ◯

Materials List:

....
....
....
....
....
....
....

Picture:

Notes:
....
....
....
....
....
....
....
....
....
....

Review:
....
....
....
....
....

Would Do Again:

Yes ◯   No ◯   Maybe ◯

Progress Tracker:

▶

Project Planner

Craft Type:

Pattern:

Date Started:

Date Ended:

Difficulty Level:

Beginner   Advanced

Materials List:

Picture:

Notes:

Review:

Would Do Again:

Yes   No   Maybe

Progress Tracker:

Project Planner

Craft Type: ....
....

Pattern: ....
....

Materials List:

....
....
....
....
....
....
....

Date Started: ....

Date Ended: ....

Difficulty Level:

Beginner   Advanced

◯ ◯ ◯ ◯ ◯

Picture:

Notes:

....
....
....
....
....
....
....
....
....
....
....
....

Review:

....
....
....
....
....
....

Would Do Again:

Yes ◯   No ◯   Maybe ◯

Progress Tracker:

▶

Project Planner

Craft Type: ....

Pattern: ....

Date Started: ....

Date Ended: ....

Materials List:
....
....
....
....
....
....

Difficulty Level:

Beginner   Advanced

◯ ◯ ◯ ◯ ◯

Picture:

Notes:
....
....
....
....
....
....
....
....
....
....
....

Review:
....
....
....
....
....
....

Would Do Again:

Yes ◯   No ◯   Maybe ◯

Progress Tracker:

▶

Project Planner

Craft Type: ....
....

Pattern: ....
....

Date Started: ....

Date Ended: ....

Difficulty Level:

Beginner   Advanced

◯ ◯ ◯ ◯ ◯

Materials List:

....
....
....
....
....
....
....

Picture:

Notes:

....
....
....
....
....
....
....
....
....
....

Review:

....
....
....
....
....

Would Do Again:

Yes ◯   No ◯   Maybe ◯

Progress Tracker:

▶

Project Planner

Craft Type: ....

....

Pattern: ....

....

Materials List:

....

....

....

....

....

....

....

Date Started: ....

Date Ended: ....

Difficulty Level:

Beginner   Advanced

◯ ◯ ◯ ◯ ◯

Picture:

Notes:

....

....

....

....

....

....

....

....

....

....

....

Review:

....

....

....

....

....

Would Do Again:

Yes ◯   No ◯   Maybe ◯

Progress Tracker:

▶

Project Planner

Craft Type: ....

Pattern: ....

....

Materials List:

....
....
....
....
....
....
....

Date Started: ....

Date Ended: ....

Difficulty Level:

Beginner   Advanced

◯ ◯ ◯ ◯ ◯

Picture:

Notes:

....
....
....
....
....
....
....
....
....
....
....

Review:

....
....
....
....
....

Would Do Again:

Yes ◯   No ◯   Maybe ◯

Progress Tracker:

▶

Project Planner

Craft Type: ....

....

Pattern: ....

....

Date Started: ....

Date Ended: ....

Difficulty Level:

Beginner   Advanced

○   ○   ○   ○   ○

Materials List:

....

....

....

....

....

....

....

Picture:

Notes:

....

....

....

....

....

....

....

....

....

....

....

Review:

....

....

....

....

....

....

Would Do Again:

Yes ○   No ○   Maybe ○

Progress Tracker:

Project Planner

Craft Type: ....

....

Pattern: ....

....

Date Started: ....

Date Ended: ....

Difficulty Level:

Beginner   Advanced

◯ ◯ ◯ ◯ ◯

Materials List:

....

....

....

....

....

....

....

Picture:

Notes:

Review:

....

....

....

....

....

Would Do Again:

Yes ◯   No ◯   Maybe ◯

Progress Tracker:

▶

Project Planner

Craft Type: ....

....

Pattern: ....

....

Materials List:

....

....

....

....

....

....

Notes:

Date Started: ....

Date Ended: ....

Difficulty Level:

Beginner   Advanced

◯ ◯ ◯ ◯ ◯

Picture:

Review:

....

....

....

....

....

....

Would Do Again:

Yes ◯   No ◯   Maybe ◯

Progress Tracker:

▶

Project Planner

Craft Type: ....
....

Pattern: ....
....

Date Started: ....

Date Ended: ....

Difficulty Level:

Beginner   Advanced

◯   ◯   ◯   ◯   ◯

Materials List:

....
....
....
....
....
....
....

Picture:

Notes:

....
....
....
....
....
....
....
....
....
....

Review:

....
....
....
....
....

Would Do Again:

Yes ◯   No ◯   Maybe ◯

Progress Tracker:

▶

Project Planner

Craft Type: ....
....

Pattern: ....
....

Materials List:
....
....
....
....
....
....
....

Date Started: ....

Date Ended: ....

Difficulty Level:

Beginner   Advanced
◯   ◯   ◯   ◯   ◯

Picture:

Notes:
....
....
....
....
....
....
....
....
....
....
....

Review:
....
....
....
....
....

Would Do Again:

Yes ◯   No ◯   Maybe ◯

Progress Tracker:

▶

Project Planner

Craft Type: ....

....

Pattern: ....

....

Date Started: ....

Date Ended: ....

Difficulty Level:

Beginner   Advanced

◯ ◯ ◯ ◯ ◯

Materials List:

....

....

....

....

....

....

....

Picture:

Notes:

....

....

....

....

....

....

....

....

....

....

....

....

Review:

....

....

....

....

....

Would Do Again:

Yes ◯   No ◯   Maybe ◯

Progress Tracker:

▶

Project Planner

Craft Type: ....
....

Pattern: ....
....

Materials List:

....
....
....
....
....
....
....

Date Started: ....

Date Ended: ....

Difficulty Level:

Beginner   Advanced

◯ ◯ ◯ ◯ ◯

Picture:

Notes:

Review:

Would Do Again:

Yes ◯   No ◯   Maybe ◯

Progress Tracker:

▶

Project Planner

Craft Type: ....

....

Pattern: ....

....

Date Started: ....

Date Ended: ....

Difficulty Level:

Beginner   Advanced

◯ ◯ ◯ ◯ ◯

Materials List:

....

....

....

....

....

....

....

Picture:

Notes:

....

....

....

....

....

....

....

....

....

....

Review:

....

....

....

....

....

....

Would Do Again:

Yes ◯   No ◯   Maybe ◯

Progress Tracker:

Project Planner

Craft Type: ....
....

Pattern: ....
....

Materials List:
....
....
....
....
....
....

Date Started: ....

Date Ended: ....

Difficulty Level:

Beginner   Advanced

◯ ◯ ◯ ◯ ◯

Picture:

Notes:
....
....
....
....
....
....
....
....
....
....
....

Review:
....
....
....
....
....

Would Do Again:

Yes ◯   No ◯   Maybe ◯

Progress Tracker:

▶

54

Project Planner

Craft Type: ....

....

Pattern: ....

....

Date Started: ....

Date Ended: ....

Difficulty Level:

Beginner   Advanced

◯   ◯   ◯   ◯   ◯

Materials List:

....

....

....

....

....

....

....

Picture:

Notes:

....

....

....

....

....

....

....

....

....

....

....

Review:

....

....

....

....

....

Would Do Again:

Yes ◯   No ◯   Maybe ◯

Progress Tracker:

▶

Project Planner

Craft Type: ....

....

Pattern: ....

....

Date Started: ....

Date Ended: ....

Difficulty Level:

Beginner   Advanced

◯ ◯ ◯ ◯ ◯

Materials List:

....

....

....

....

....

....

....

Picture:

Notes:

....

....

....

....

....

....

....

....

....

....

....

Review:

....

....

....

....

....

Would Do Again:

Yes ◯   No ◯   Maybe ◯

Progress Tracker:

▶

Project Planner

Craft Type: ....
....

Pattern: ....
....

Materials List:
....
....
....
....
....
....
....

Notes:

Progress Tracker:

Date Started: ....

Date Ended: ....

Difficulty Level:

Beginner   Advanced
◯   ◯   ◯   ◯   ◯

Picture:

Review:
....
....
....
....
....

Would Do Again:

Yes ◯   No ◯   Maybe ◯

Project Planner

Craft Type: ....
....

Pattern: ....
....

Materials List:
....
....
....
....
....
....
....

Notes:
....
....
....
....
....
....
....
....
....
....
....
....
....

Progress Tracker:

Date Started: ....

Date Ended: ....

Difficulty Level:

Beginner   Advanced

Picture:

Review:
....
....
....
....
....
....

Would Do Again:

Yes   No   Maybe

58

Project Planner

Craft Type: ....

....

Pattern: ....

....

Date Started: ....

Date Ended: ....

Difficulty Level:

Beginner   Advanced

◯   ◯   ◯   ◯   ◯

Materials List:

....

....

....

....

....

....

....

Picture:

Notes:

....

....

....

....

....

....

....

....

....

....

....

....

....

....

Review:

....

....

....

....

....

....

Would Do Again:

Yes ◯   No ◯   Maybe ◯

Progress Tracker:

▶

Project Planner

Craft Type: ....

....

Pattern: ....

....

Date Started: ....

Date Ended: ....

Difficulty Level:

Beginner   Advanced

◯ ◯ ◯ ◯ ◯

Materials List:

....
....
....
....
....
....
....

Picture:

Notes:

....
....
....
....
....
....
....
....
....
....
....
....
....

Review:

....
....
....
....
....

Would Do Again:

Yes ◯   No ◯   Maybe ◯

Progress Tracker:

▶

Project Planner

Craft Type: ....

....

Pattern: ....

....

Date Started: ....

Date Ended: ....

Difficulty Level:

Beginner   Advanced

○ ○ ○ ○ ○

Materials List:

....
....
....
....
....
....
....

Picture:

Notes:

....
....
....
....
....
....
....
....
....
....

Review:

....
....
....
....
....

Would Do Again:

Yes ○   No ○   Maybe ○

Progress Tracker:

▶

Project Planner

Craft Type: ....

....

Pattern: ....

....

Date Started: ....

Date Ended: ....

Difficulty Level:

Beginner   Advanced

◯ ◯ ◯ ◯ ◯

Materials List:

....

....

....

....

....

....

Picture:

Notes:

....

....

....

....

....

....

....

....

....

....

....

....

Review:

....

....

....

....

....

Would Do Again:

Yes ◯   No ◯   Maybe ◯

Progress Tracker:

Project Planner

Craft Type: ....

....

Pattern: ....

....

Materials List:

....

....

....

....

....

....

....

Date Started: ....

Date Ended: ....

Difficulty Level:

Beginner   Advanced

◯ ◯ ◯ ◯ ◯

Picture:

Notes:

....

....

....

....

....

....

....

....

....

....

....

Review:

....

....

....

....

....

Would Do Again:

Yes ◯   No ◯   Maybe ◯

Progress Tracker:

▶

Project Planner

Craft Type: ....
....

Pattern: ....
....

Materials List:
....
....
....
....
....
....
....

Notes:
....
....
....
....
....
....
....
....
....
....
....

Progress Tracker:

Date Started: ....

Date Ended: ....

Difficulty Level:

Beginner   Advanced

◯ ◯ ◯ ◯ ◯

Picture:

Review:
....
....
....
....
....
....

Would Do Again:

Yes ◯   No ◯   Maybe ◯

64

Project Planner

Craft Type: ....

....

Pattern: ....

....

Materials List:

....
....
....
....
....
....
....

Date Started: ....

Date Ended: ....

Difficulty Level:

Beginner   Advanced

◯ ◯ ◯ ◯ ◯

Picture:

Notes:

....
....
....
....
....
....
....
....
....
....
....

Review:

....
....
....
....
....

Would Do Again:

Yes ◯   No ◯   Maybe ◯

Progress Tracker:

▶

Project Planner

Craft Type: ....
....

Pattern: ....
....

Date Started: ....

Date Ended: ....

Difficulty Level:

Beginner   Advanced

◯ ◯ ◯ ◯ ◯

Materials List:
....
....
....
....
....
....

Picture:

Notes:
....
....
....
....
....
....
....
....
....
....
....
....

Review:
....
....
....
....
....
....

Would Do Again:

Yes ◯   No ◯   Maybe ◯

Progress Tracker:

Project Planner

Craft Type: ....

....

Pattern: ....

....

Materials List:

....

....

....

....

....

....

....

Difficulty Level:

Beginner   Advanced

◯ ◯ ◯ ◯ ◯

Picture:

Notes:

....

....

....

....

....

....

....

....

....

....

....

Review:

....

....

....

....

....

....

Would Do Again:

Yes ◯   No ◯   Maybe ◯

Progress Tracker:

Project Planner

Craft Type: ....

....

Pattern: ....

....

Date Started: ....

Date Ended: ....

Difficulty Level:

Beginner   Advanced

◯ ◯ ◯ ◯ ◯

Materials List:

....

....

....

....

....

....

....

Picture:

Notes:

....

....

....

....

....

....

....

....

....

....

Review:

....

....

....

....

....

....

Would Do Again:

Yes ◯   No ◯   Maybe ◯

Progress Tracker:

▶

Project Planner

Craft Type: ....

....

Pattern: ....

....

Date Started: ....

Date Ended: ....

Difficulty Level:

Beginner   Advanced

◯ ◯ ◯ ◯ ◯

Materials List:

....

....

....

....

....

....

Picture:

Notes:

....

....

....

....

....

....

....

....

....

Review:

....

....

....

....

....

Would Do Again:

Yes ◯   No ◯   Maybe ◯

Progress Tracker:

Project Planner

Craft Type: ....

....

Pattern: ....

....

Date Started: ....

Date Ended: ....

Difficulty Level:

Beginner   Advanced

Materials List:

....

....

....

....

....

....

....

Picture:

Notes:

....

....

....

....

....

....

....

....

....

....

....

Review:

....

....

....

....

....

....

Would Do Again:

Yes   No   Maybe

Progress Tracker:

Project Planner

Craft Type: ....
....

Pattern: ....
....

Date Started: ....

Date Ended: ....

Difficulty Level:

Beginner   Advanced

◯ ◯ ◯ ◯ ◯

Materials List:
....
....
....
....
....
....
....

Picture:

Notes:
....
....
....
....
....
....
....
....
....
....
....

Review:
....
....
....
....
....

Would Do Again:

Yes ◯   No ◯   Maybe ◯

Progress Tracker:

▶

Project Planner

Craft Type: ....
....

Pattern: ....
....

Date Started: ....
Date Ended: ....

Difficulty Level:

Beginner   Advanced
◯ ◯ ◯ ◯ ◯

Materials List:
....
....
....
....
....
....

Picture:

Notes:
....
....
....
....
....
....
....
....
....
....
....

Review:
....
....
....
....

Would Do Again:

Yes ◯   No ◯   Maybe ◯

Progress Tracker:

▶

Project Planner

Craft Type: ....
....

Pattern: ....
....

Date Started: ....

Date Ended: ....

Difficulty Level:

Beginner   Advanced

◯ ◯ ◯ ◯ ◯

Materials List:

....
....
....
....
....
....
....

Picture:

Notes:

....
....
....
....
....
....
....
....
....
....

Review:

....
....
....
....
....

Would Do Again:

Yes ◯   No ◯   Maybe ◯

Progress Tracker:

Project Planner

Craft Type: ....

....

Pattern: ....

....

Date Started: ....

Date Ended: ....

Difficulty Level:

Beginner   Advanced

◯ ◯ ◯ ◯ ◯

Materials List:

....

....

....

....

....

....

....

Picture:

Notes:

....

....

....

....

....

....

....

....

....

....

....

....

Review:

....

....

....

....

....

....

Would Do Again:

Yes ◯   No ◯   Maybe ◯

Progress Tracker:

Project Planner

Craft Type: ....

....

Pattern: ....

....

Date Started: ....

Date Ended: ....

Difficulty Level:

Beginner   Advanced

◯ ◯ ◯ ◯ ◯

Materials List:

....

....

....

....

....

....

Picture:

Notes:

....

....

....

....

....

....

....

....

....

....

....

....

Review:

....

....

....

....

....

Would Do Again:

Yes ◯   No ◯   Maybe ◯

Progress Tracker:

▶

Project Planner

Craft Type: ....
....

Pattern: ....
....

Materials List:

....
....
....
....
....
....
....

Notes:

Date Started: ....

Date Ended: ....

Difficulty Level:

Beginner   Advanced

◯   ◯   ◯   ◯   ◯

Picture:

Review:

....
....
....
....
....
....

Would Do Again:

Yes ◯   No ◯   Maybe ◯

Progress Tracker:

▶

Project Planner

Craft Type: ....
....
Pattern: ....
....

Date Started: ....
Date Ended: ....

Difficulty Level:

Beginner   Advanced

◯ ◯ ◯ ◯ ◯

Materials List:

....
....
....
....
....
....
....

Picture:

Notes:

....
....
....
....
....
....
....
....
....
....

Review:

....
....
....
....
....

Would Do Again:

Yes ◯   No ◯   Maybe ◯

Progress Tracker:

Project Planner

Craft Type: ....
....

Pattern: ....
....

Materials List:

Date Started: ....

Date Ended: ....

Difficulty Level:

Beginner   Advanced

◯ ◯ ◯ ◯ ◯

Picture:

Notes:

Review:

Would Do Again:

Yes ◯   No ◯   Maybe ◯

Progress Tracker:

Project Planner

Craft Type: ....
....

Pattern: ....
....

Date Started: ....

Date Ended: ....

Difficulty Level:

Beginner   Advanced

◯ ◯ ◯ ◯ ◯

Materials List:

....
....
....
....
....
....

Picture:

Notes:

....
....
....
....
....
....
....
....
....
....
....

Review:

....
....
....
....
....

Would Do Again:

Yes ◯   No ◯   Maybe ◯

Progress Tracker:

▶

Project Planner

Craft Type: ....
....

Pattern: ....
....

Materials List:

....
....
....
....
....
....

Notes:

....
....
....
....
....
....
....
....
....
....
....
....

Progress Tracker:

Date Started: ....

Date Ended: ....

Difficulty Level:

Beginner   Advanced

◯ ◯ ◯ ◯ ◯

Picture:

Review:

....
....
....
....
....

Would Do Again:

Yes ◯   No ◯   Maybe ◯

Project Planner

Craft Type: ....
....
Pattern: ....
....

Date Started: ....
Date Ended: ....

Difficulty Level:

Beginner   Advanced

◯ ◯ ◯ ◯ ◯

Materials List:
....
....
....
....
....
....

Picture:

Notes:
....
....
....
....
....
....
....
....
....
....
....
....

Review:
....
....
....
....
....

Would Do Again:

Yes ◯   No ◯   Maybe ◯

Progress Tracker:

▶

Project Planner

Craft Type: ....
....

Pattern: ....
....

Date Started: ....

Date Ended: ....

Materials List:

....
....
....
....
....
....
....

Difficulty Level:

Beginner   Advanced

◯ ◯ ◯ ◯ ◯

Picture:

Notes:

....
....
....
....
....
....
....
....
....
....
....

Review:

....
....
....
....
....
....

Would Do Again:

Yes ◯   No ◯   Maybe ◯

Progress Tracker:

Project Planner

Craft Type: ....
....
Pattern: ....
....

Date Started: ....
Date Ended: ....

Difficulty Level:

Beginner   Advanced

( )   ( )   ( )   ( )   ( )

Materials List:

....
....
....
....
....
....
....

Picture:

Notes:

....
....
....
....
....
....
....
....
....
....
....
....
....

Review:

....
....
....
....
....
....

Would Do Again:

Yes ( )   No ( )   Maybe ( )

Progress Tracker:

▶

Project Planner

Craft Type: ....
....

Pattern: ....
....

Date Started: ....

Date Ended: ....

Materials List:
....
....
....
....
....
....
....

Difficulty Level:

Beginner   Advanced

◯ ◯ ◯ ◯ ◯

Picture:

Notes:
....
....
....
....
....
....
....
....
....
....
....
....

Review:
....
....
....
....
....

Would Do Again:

Yes ◯   No ◯   Maybe ◯

Progress Tracker:

Project Planner

Craft Type: ....
....

Pattern: ....
....

Date Started: ....

Date Ended: ....

Difficulty Level:

Beginner   Advanced

◯ ◯ ◯ ◯ ◯

Materials List:

....
....
....
....
....
....
....

Picture:

Notes:
....
....
....
....
....
....
....
....
....
....
....
....

Review:
....
....
....
....
....
....

Would Do Again:

Yes ◯   No ◯   Maybe ◯

Progress Tracker:

▶

Project Planner

Craft Type: ....

....

Pattern: ....

....

Materials List:

....
....
....
....
....
....
....

Notes:

....
....
....
....
....
....
....
....
....
....
....

Progress Tracker:

Date Started: ....

Date Ended: ....

Difficulty Level:

Beginner   Advanced

◯ ◯ ◯ ◯ ◯

Picture:

Review:

....
....
....
....
....

Would Do Again:

Yes ◯   No ◯   Maybe ◯

Project Planner

Craft Type: ....
....
Pattern: ....
....

Date Started: ....
Date Ended: ....

Difficulty Level:

Beginner   Advanced

◯   ◯   ◯   ◯   ◯

Materials List:

....
....
....
....
....
....

Picture:

Notes:

....
....
....
....
....
....
....
....
....

Review:

....
....
....
....
....

Would Do Again:

Yes ◯   No ◯   Maybe ◯

Progress Tracker:

▶

Project Planner

Craft Type: ....

....

Pattern: ....

....

Materials List:

....

....

....

....

....

....

....

Date Started: ....

Date Ended: ....

Difficulty Level:

Beginner   Advanced

○ ○ ○ ○ ○

Picture:

Notes:

....

....

....

....

....

....

....

....

....

....

....

....

Review:

....

....

....

....

....

Would Do Again:

Yes ◯   No ◯   Maybe ◯

Progress Tracker:

▶

Project Planner

Craft Type: ....

Pattern: ....
....

Date Started: ....

Date Ended: ....

Difficulty Level:

Beginner   Advanced

◯ ◯ ◯ ◯ ◯

Materials List:
....
....
....
....
....
....
....

Picture:

Notes:
....
....
....
....
....
....
....
....
....
....
....

Review:
....
....
....
....
....

Would Do Again:

Yes ◯   No ◯   Maybe ◯

Progress Tracker:

▶

Project Planner

Craft Type: ....
....

Pattern: ....
....

Materials List:
....
....
....
....
....
....

Date Started: ....

Date Ended: ....

Difficulty Level:

Beginner   Advanced

◯ ◯ ◯ ◯ ◯

Picture:

Notes:
....
....
....
....
....
....
....
....
....
....
....

Review:
....
....
....
....
....

Would Do Again:

Yes ◯   No ◯   Maybe ◯

Progress Tracker:

▶

Project Planner

Craft Type: ....
....

Pattern: ....
....

Materials List:
....
....
....
....
....
....
....

Date Started: ....

Date Ended: ....

Difficulty Level:

Beginner   Advanced

◯ ◯ ◯ ◯ ◯

Picture:

Notes:
....
....
....
....
....
....
....
....
....
....
....
....

Review:
....
....
....
....
....
....

Would Do Again:

Yes ◯   No ◯   Maybe ◯

Progress Tracker:

▶

Project Planner

Craft Type: ....
....

Pattern: ....
....

Date Started: ....
Date Ended: ....

Difficulty Level:

Beginner   Advanced

◯ ◯ ◯ ◯ ◯

Materials List:

....
....
....
....
....
....
....

Picture:

Notes:

....
....
....
....
....
....
....
....
....
....

Review:

....
....
....
....
....

Would Do Again:

Yes ◯   No ◯   Maybe ◯

Progress Tracker:

Project Planner

Craft Type: ....

....

Pattern: ....

....

Date Started: ....

Date Ended: ....

Difficulty Level:

Beginner   Advanced

◯ ◯ ◯ ◯ ◯

Materials List:

....
....
....
....
....
....

Picture:

Notes:

....
....
....
....
....
....
....
....
....
....

Review:

....
....
....
....
....

Would Do Again:

Yes ◯   No ◯   Maybe ◯

Progress Tracker:

▶

Project Planner

Craft Type: ....
....

Pattern: ....
....

Date Started: ....

Date Ended: ....

Difficulty Level:

Beginner   Advanced
◯   ◯   ◯   ◯   ◯

Materials List:
....
....
....
....
....
....
....

Picture:

Notes:
....
....
....
....
....
....
....
....
....
....

Review:
....
....
....
....
....
....

Would Do Again:

Yes ◯   No ◯   Maybe ◯

Progress Tracker:

▶